T0011826

THE LITTLE BOOK OF
COUNTRY

Published in 2023 by OH!
An imprint of Welbeck Non-Fiction Limited, part of Welbeck Publishing Group.
Offices in London, 20 Mortimer Street, London W1T 3JW,
and Sydney, 205 Commonwealth Street, Surry Hills 2010
www.welbeckpublishing.com

A CIP catalogue record for this book is available from the British Library.

ISBN 978-1-83861-139-2

Associate Publisher: Lisa Dyer
Compiled and written by: Theresa Bebbington
Design: Andy Jones, Topics – The Creative Partnership
Production: Felicity Awdry

Printed and bound in Dubai

10 9 8 7 6 5 4 3 2 1

THE LITTLE BOOK OF
COUNTRY

The history, hits, and heartaches

CONTENTS
• • • • • • • • • • • •

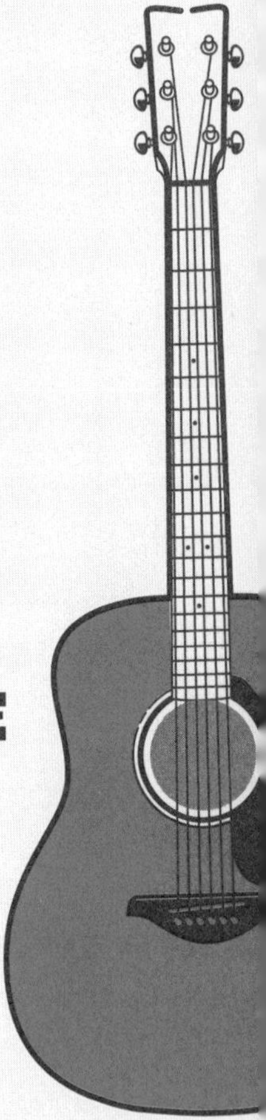

INTRODUCTION

From the early beginnings of folk balladeers, bluegrass fiddlers, and cowboy yodelers through to classic crooners Hank Williams and Johnny Cash to modern stars Shania Twain and Keith Urban, this little book introduces you to the key musicians, music styles, and moments in country history.

In chapter one, Country's Roots, we journey back through history to European folk music and Appalachian jug bands and bluegrass, charting the very first country music coming out of the U.S.A. Learn about singing cowboys like Gene Autry and Roy Rogers and different styles of country music, from honky-tonk to Southern rock, in the second chapter, The Many Sounds of Country. Take a trip to Nashville and music venues in It

Happens Here; stop by the Grand Ole Opry
or do some line-dancing at Austin's Broken
Spoke. In The Hits and Hitmakers, you'll
celebrate the scores of famous No. 1 songs
and the even more famous singers, while
chapter five, Banjos, Guitars, and More,
gives you the lowdown on the essential
sounds that make country country, as well
as legendary instruments, such as Clarence
White's Martin D-28 and Maybelle Carter's
Gibson L-5. Finally, Hearts on Sleeves offers
words of wisdom, life advice, and thoughts
on country music from the most talented
performers ever to walk the earth.

If you're planning to visit a country hot-spot
or festival, or just want to brush up on your
music knowledge, this book will get you
cranking up the country on high volume.

★ ★ ★ ★ ★ ★ ★ ★ ★ ★

CHAPTER 1

COUNTRY'S ROOTS

Learn how folk, fiddle, and gospel
music became country, with
other genres giving a helping
hand along the way.

★ ★ ★ ★ ★ ★ ★ ★ ★ ★

HOW TO DEFINE COUNTRY MUSIC

Whether you call it country music, country and western, or simply country, here's a definition of one of America's most popular genres of music from Merriam-Webster:

"Music derived from or imitating the folk style of the Southern U.S. or of the Western cowboy . . . especially: popular vocal music characterized by simple harmonies, accompaniment by stringed instruments (such as guitar, fiddle, banjo, and pedal steel), repeated choruses, and often narrative lyrics."

FOLK VERSUS COUNTRY

Although both have similar subject themes about the singer's life, loves, and loss, folk is generally known as more acoustic and based on traditional melodies, while country music includes elements of rock and blues.

AURAL TRADITION

Folk songs were once passed down from one generation to the next, with the music being played on traditional acoustic instruments. Rather than reading music or lyrics written on paper, the new generations would have to learn the lyrics and how to play the instruments by listening to their relatives or friends perform.

THE COMMON PEOPLE

The word *folk* comes from an Old English word that means "common people," which was taken from the Old High German *folc*, first used in the 12th century. A British dictionary describes folk music as "music that originates in traditional popular culture or is written in that style."

66

COUNTRY MUSIC IS THE
PEOPLE'S MUSIC. IT JUST
SPEAKS ABOUT REAL LIFE
AND ABOUT TRUTH AND IT
TELLS THINGS HOW THEY
REALLY ARE.

FAITH HILL
Singer

FOLK MUSIC AROUND THE WORLD

France: *Musique populaire*, meaning "popular music," is music associated with a social class, the "folk."

Italy: *Musica poplare*, meaning "popular music," is also music associated with a social class, the "folk."

Germany: *Volksmusik*, meaning "people's music," combines class with an ethnic group.

India: *Log git*, for the Hindi language, meaning "the people's music," also combines class with an ethnic group.

Czech Republic (*and some other Slavic countries*): *Narod*, meaning "nation," is a music that unites people in the country.

Iran: *Musiqi-ye mahalli,* meaning "regional music," refers to there being distinct folk styles in different regions.

Source: www.britannica.com

ECCLESIASTICAL INFLUENCE

1

When Christianity expanded in medieval Europe, folk music was linked to heathen rites and customs, so the Church tried to suppressed it. However, it was assimilated into liturgical music, which in turn was assimilated into folk music. By the 16th century, folk music returned to popularity among the literate urban class and some folk songs can be found in Renaissance manuscripts.

FOLK STYLES
1

Béla Bartók (1881–1945)
One of Hungary's greatest composers,
and an ethnomusicologist, he would
use a phonograph to record peasants
singing folk songs. He named two
principle singing styles in European
folk: *parlando-rubato* and *tempo giusto*.

Parlando-rubato
This style stresses the words, is highly
ornamented, and often departs from
strict metric and rhythmic patterns.

Tempo giusto
This style has an even tempo and
follows metric patterns.

FOLK STYLES II

The American folk music scholar Alan Lomax (1915–2002) also made numerous field recordings of folk music. He named three distinct singing styles: Eurasian, Old European, and modern European.

Eurasian: A style noted for tense, ornamented, usually solo singing, is found in southern Europe and in parts of Great Britain and Ireland, as well as in South Asia and the Middle East.

Old European: A more relaxed sound that is created with a full voice and is often used by a group of singers blending their voices. It is prominent in central, eastern, and parts of northern Europe.

Modern European: This style is a combination of the other two and is mostly found in western Europe and urban areas.

MONOPHONIC BEGINNINGS

Traditional folk music from rural areas is often monophonic, meaning it has only one melodic line. However, polyphonic folk music, with a number of concurrent melodic lines, also forms part of traditional folk music in some regions of the world and is now common in 21st-century commercial and urban folk music.

ECCLESIASTICAL INFLUENCE II

In creating church music, religious texts have, at various times in history, been combined with secular folk tunes. This can be seen in the hymns of the Protestant Reformation. And in the 19th century, revival hymns—known as folk hymns because of their links with folklike groups—were part of American camp meetings.

APPALACHIAN FOLK

When people immigrate, their music travels with them. People from England, Scotland, Ireland, and other parts of Europe settled in the Appalachian Mountains in eastern parts of the United States in the 18th and 19th centuries. They brought their traditional folk ballads and songs, along with their instruments, with them.

THE BIRTH OF COUNTRY

Immigrant settlers in the Appalachians may have been shielded from outside influences by the mountains, but with the expansion of the railroad during the Civil War, they were introduced to rhythmic blues music sung by slaves and railroad workers, as well as to the music of touring vaudeville acts and minstrel troupes.

Early country music was
founded on the fiddle, the
accordion, the banjo, and
the autoharp. Appalachian-
based bluegrass traditionally
included the use of the zither
and the mandolin, while a "jug
band" contained the bass
or bull fiddle, a washboard,
and the harmonica
(or mouth organ).

In the 1920s, country songs were known as Old Familiar Tunes. As the listening audience expanded, songs became known as Old-Time Melodies of the Sunny South or Hill Country Songs and Ballads. Simple in form and harmony, they were mostly romantic or melancholic ballads derived from a mix of songs and music from British ballads, African-American blues, and church music.

> "

WE HAVE THAT STORYTELLING
HISTORY IN COUNTRY AND
BLUEGRASS AND OLD TIME AND
FOLK MUSIC, BLUES—ALL THOSE
THINGS THAT COMBINE TO MAKE
UP THE GENRE. IT WAS PROBABLY
STORYTELLING BEFORE IT WAS
SONGWRITING, AS FAR AS
COUNTRY MUSIC IS CONCERNED.

"

CHRIS STAPLETON
Singer-songwriter, guitarist, and record producer

EVERYBODY'S LIFE IS A SOAP OPERA. EVERYBODY'S LIFE IS A COUNTRY-WESTERN SONG, DEPENDS ON WHO'S WRITING IT.

DOLLY PARTON
BBC interview, February 2019

EARLY RECORDINGS

With new technology available in the late 19th century to mechanically record music and print it, and Edison's phonograph, folk music became more easily accessible. The first country music recordings of Appalachian fiddle players were made in the late 1910s, and the genre started to gain its feet by the early 1920s.

COUNTRY MUSIC'S BIRTHPLACE

The United States Congress passed a resolution in 1998 that recognized Bristol, Tennessee, as the "birthplace of country music." With the introduction of remote recording in 1927, Ralph Peer decided to travel to the Appalachias, where he set up in Bristol to make his now-famous recordings (see page 68).

INTRODUCING COUNTRY TO THE COUNTRY

With the advent of recording, music could be enjoyed by people at home, and country music soon could be heard on the radio. The point in history considered to mark the "moment country was born" is when Victor Records recorded Jimmie Rodgers and the Carter Family in 1927.

THE FIRST COUNTRY RADIO STATION

Before TV, families would sit around the radio to listen to music and other programs. One of the most popular, broadcast from Nashville, Tennessee, was a live country-music variety show: the *Grand Ole Opry*. Listeners could hear old-time music as well as western music.

TOP 10 COUNTRIES FOR COUNTRY

According to the Country Radio Seminar 2022, here are the top 10 countries for streaming country music through YouTube;

1. **United States: 62.9%**
2. **Canada: 5.7%**
3. **United Kingdom: 2.9%**
4. **Philippines: 2.8%**
5. **Brazil: 2.5%**
6. **Australia: 2.3%**
7. **Mexico: 1.9%**
8. **India: 1.3%**
9. **Germany: 1.2%**
10. **Indonesia: 1.0%**

NO. 1 IN THE U.S.A.

According to demographics, country music was the No. 1 format for adults in the 18–54 age group in 2016. Of the 2,000-plus radio stations on air at the time, it was also the top radio format.

CHAPTER 2

THE MANY SOUNDS OF COUNTRY

Most people associate country music with cowboys, but there's so much more to it than that, from the country yodel to bro-country.

WHAT MAKES COUNTRY COUNTRY?

Over the decades country music has created an infinite number of different sounds and styles, yet there are several main elements that always unite them:

1. Folk harmonies, based on traditional, simple chord progressions.
2. The musician or members of a band play string instruments, such as guitar, bass, banjo, and fiddle.
3. The voice must have a twang!
4. Storytelling confessional lyrics are about love, heartache, and pain.
5. Dueting (though not essential) is often a prominent feature.

Source: www.masterclass.com

COUNTRY YODEL

Jimmie Rodgers had worked in railroad gangs where African-Americans sang work chants, and he combined old-time music and folk in his own songs. His first hit record, "Blue Yodel," featured a vocal technique called yodeling in which he would sing while quickly changing from a high to normal voice. It sold almost half a million records in 1927.

> **THE TRADITIONAL COUNTRY MUSIC STAYS BECAUSE IT'S SUCH AN ALL-AROUND GOOD FORMAT AND IT'S FUN TO WRITE SONGS LIKE 'OH SUSANNAH.' I JUST FEEL ALONG WITH THAT YOU GOTTA TALK ABOUT WHAT'S GOING ON TODAY.**

EDDIE RABBITT
Country music singer-songwriter

According to
market research by the
NPD Group, country music
became the United States'
favorite music genre
in 2012, when it finally
beat classic rock across
all age demographics.

RIDE 'EM COWBOY

In the 1930s and '40s, western music that featured a horselike clippity-clop rhythm became popular. The songs' lyrics are often about lovesick cowboys and gun-fighting bandits. The music style traveled from the radio to the big screen, with singing cowboys appearing in Hollywood cowboy movies.

SINGING COWBOY STARS

Two singing cowboys in the early
western movies became huge stars:
Gene Autry and Roy Rogers. Picking
up on their popularity, Nashville
executives did away with the hillbilly
image associated with old-time music
and pushed the cowboy to the forefront.
They dressed their musicians in cowboy
gear and gave the genre a new name:
country and western.

IF I'M WRITING SONGS FOR A COUNTRY-WESTERN PICTURE, I HAVE TO KNOW ABOUT COUNTRY MUSIC.

HENRY MANCINI
Composer and conductor

COUNTRY AND JAZZ MASH-UP

Texas, Oklahoma, and California would become home to a new dance music style: western swing. This lively music combined western country music with swing jazz, and the instruments, such as pedal steel guitars, were amplified so they could be heard in large dance hall venues. Bob Wills and The Texas Playboys were popular western swing bands.

"

I THINK RAY CHARLES DID
AS MUCH AS ANYBODY
WHEN HE DID HIS COUNTRY
MUSIC ALBUM. RAY
CHARLES BROKE DOWN
BORDERS AND SHOWED
THE SIMILARITIES BETWEEN
COUNTRY MUSIC AND R&B.

"

WILLIE NELSON
Musician and singer-songwriter

ROCKING ROCKABILLY

When western swing bands started to perform R&B songs along with country songs, they developed another music style known as rockabilly. Typical rockabilly instruments included an acoustic guitar, electric guitar, stand-up bass, and drums. Hits came from such musicians as Elvis Presley, Carl Perkins, Roy Orbison, and Johnny Cash.

WHAT IS A HONKY-TONK?

The word *honky-tonk* first appeared in the late 19th century and referred to a "dive" or "a cheap nightclub or bar" and "especially one that features country music." It also referred to a ragtime-style of piano-playing performed in such bars, and as a type of country music "that has a heavy beat and lyrics dealing usually with vice or misfortune."

TEXAS TUNES

In the 1940s, when mainstream country was becoming commercialized, musicians turned to a more authentic new style of music known as honky-tonk, named after the working-class bars that could be found near oil fields in Texas. These bands normally included pedal steel and acoustic guitars, fiddle, stand-up bass, and drums.

WORKING-CLASS TROUBLE

Honky-tonk music was popular among the working class, who could relate to the struggles voiced through the lyrics. One of the most popular singers was Hank Williams. Unfortunately, the singer had a short, troubled life, marred by drinking, and died at just 29 years of age. Regardless, he wrote hundreds of well-loved country classics, including "Cold Cold Heart," and "I'm So Lonesome I Could Cry."

Hank Williams' "Honky Tonkin'" went to No. 14 on *Billboard* in 1948. In 1982 it became the sixth No. 1 single for his son, Hank Williams Jr.

AFRICAN-AMERICAN CONTRIBUTIONS

Country music would not have been the same without the influence of African-Americans, yet there has been little recognition of their efforts. The Country Music Foundation set out to rectify this in 1998 when they released with Warner Brothers a three-CD package *From Where I Stand: The Black Experience in Country Music.*

HARMONIOUS BLUEGRASS

The 1940s saw a revival of old-time music with Bill Monroe and the Blue Grass Boys playing bluegrass. Based on old-time Appalachian music, bluegrass featured a number of string instruments, such as guitar, banjo, mandolin, fiddle, and bass, and usually two to four singers would sing in harmony. The style was revived a second time in the 1970s, when the Nitty Gritty Dirt Band was popular.

THE COUNTRY BALLAD

In the mid-1950s, Nashville record producers, such as Chet Atkins, came up with the country ballad to draw rock n' roll listeners to country. They recorded sweet ballads sung by Patsy Cline, Tammy Wynette, George Jones, and Jim Reeves, among others, using orchestral strings and choirs instead of the usual fiddle, guitar, and banjo.

CLASSIC COUNTRY

Radio stations tend to refer to country hits that have managed to get air play over several decades as "classic country." This includes the golden age of the 1920s to 1970s, from Hank Williams, George Jones, and Johnny Cash, and a second category from 1960s to the 1990s, including Waylon Jennings, Merle Haggard, George Strait, and Garth Brooks.

OUTLAWED

Outlaw country was born when some 1960s country musicians steered toward a more progressive sound. Based in Nashville, Willie Nelson, Waylon Jennings, Kris Kristofferson, and Johnny Cash added progressive strands from folk music along with rockabilly to create the new style. The same four men would later form The Highwaymen.

THE BAKERSFIELD SOUND

Between the 1940s and 1960s, Bakersfield, California, was known as the Nashville of the West as people from Texas, Arkansas, and Oklahoma came looking for work and brought their music along. Rougher, twangier, and edgier than the polished Nashville sound, the Bakersfield sound is typified by the music of Merle Haggard and Buck Owens.

A LITTLE BIT COUNTRY...

Some musicians veered between country and rock music in the mid-1960s—forming the genre known as country rock. Folk artists such as Neil Young, Gram Parsons, and Bob Dylan started adding strands of country to their sound, which can be heard in *Sweetheart of the Rodeo*, a 1968 hit album by the Byrds, which Parsons had joined.

RED DIRT

Another country style where there is a subtle mash-up with rock is known as Red Dirt. It is named for the red dirt of Stillwater, Oklahoma. Its lyrical attitude takes it away from the traditional classic country. Among artists known for their red dirt music are Cross Canadian Ragweed, Bob Childers, and Tom Skinner.

POP, POP, POP... COUNTRY POP

Not surprisingly, from the 1960s onward, with the appearance of pop music, there was a crossover into country, leading to country pop, which often has a lilting style and catchy melodies. Notable artists include Bobbie Gentry, Glen Campbell, Kenny Rogers, and Dolly Parton through to Miley Cyrus and Taylor Swift today.

THE NEW
TRADITIONALISTS

In the 1980s, country musicians rebelled
against the smooth, easy-listening
country being churned out by record
producers and went back to a more
authentic sound inspired by honky-
tonk and outlaw country. George Strait,
Randy Travis, and Dwight Yoakam are
some of the artists who were creating
"new traditionalist" music.

THE ALTERNATIVE

Not only is there alternative rock—where some groups, such as R.E.M. and Cowboy Junkies, began adding traditional country instruments, such the mandolin, to their compositions—but there's also "alt-country" in which alternative and country music styles have merged. Uncle Tupelo, Wilco, and Son Volt are among the musicians who helped develop this sound.

> **"**
>
> I GREW UP IN MOUNTAIN PINES, ARKANSAS. YOU GET NO MORE COUNTRY THAN WHERE I GREW UP. BUT I ALSO GREW UP IN THE NAPSTER / ITUNES / SPOTIFY / IHEART RADIO ERA, AND SO I SEE THAT EVERYTHING IS INFLUENCED BY EVERYTHING ELSE, AND THAT'S WHAT COUNTRY MUSIC IS NOW.
>
> **"**

BOBBY BONES

Radio and TV personality

According to research by the Country Music Association, more than 129 million, or 51%, of American adults now listen to country music, at a growth of 9% over the past five years.

SOUTHERN ROCK

More a subgenre of rock than country,
with a focus on electric guitars and
vocals, this style derived from rock,
country, and blues in the southern U.S.
in the 1970s with such bands as the
Allman Brothers, Lynyrd Skynyrd, and
ZZ Top. Some say that southern rock is
rock with a little "good-ol-boy" mixed in
and country rock is rocked-up country.

BRO-COUNTRY

Perhaps not a favorite among diehard classic country fans, the term "bro-country" refers to recent country music trends from 2010s, a style that includes elements of hip-hop, hard rock, and electronica, and lyrics that focus on subjects such as guns, partying, and pickup trucks. Florida Georgia Line, Luke Bryan, Jason Aldean, and Blake Shelton are artists whose music falls into this category.

AMERICANA

On the other side of the spectrum is
Americana music, which combines
traditional country, gospel, and blues
with working-class folk, such as in
the music by Steve Earle, Rhiannon
Giddens, The Chicks, Miranda Lambert,
and Brandi Carlile.

CHAPTER 3

IT
HAPPENS
HERE

The first home to country was in the
remote Appalachian Mountains,
but from there it spread across the
country—with Nashville becoming
the beating heart of the industry—and
continuing around the world.

THE BRISTOL SESSIONS

In 1927, Ralph Peer decided to go to the source of the country singers, and Bristol, Tennessee became a hub, where he recorded Ernest and Hattie Stoneman, Henry Whitter, the Johnson Brothers, and others. These famously became known as the Bristol Sessions.

THE CROOKED ROAD

Found in southwest Virginia, the Crooked Road is a 330-mile (530-km)-long heritage trail with 60 venues along the way in which music lovers can visit notable historic sites. Live music and dancing can be found at such places as the Floyd Country Store and the Carter Family Fold.

TAKE A ROMP TO
OWENSBORO

The home of the Bluegrass Music Hall of Fame and Museum can be found in Owensboro, Kentucky. If you plan a visit, try to coordinate it with the annual ROMP Fest, with performances from local and nationally acclaimed artists and plenty of workshops.

TOP 10 CITIES FOR STREAMING COUNTRY

Based on statistics presented at the Country Radio Seminar 2022, here are the top 10 states for streaming country music through YouTube in a month.

1. **Houston, Texas**
2. **Chicago, Illinois**
3. **Dallas, Texas**
4. **Los Angeles, California**
5. **New York, New York**
6. **Nashville, Tennessee**
7. **Denver, Colorado**
8. **Atlanta, Georgia**
9. **Seattle, Washington**
10. **Milwaukee, Wisconsin**

NASHVILLE

Nashville, Tennessee, is a city that has become synonymous with country music. Dolly Parton calls it home, as does the Country Music Hall of Fame, the Grand Ole Opry, the Ryman Auditorium (the "Mother Church of Country Music"), and the Bluebird Café. You can dance with locals in East Nashville at the American Legion Post 82.

WHEN I FIRST CAME TO NASHVILLE, PEOPLE HARDLY GAVE COUNTRY MUSIC ANY RESPECT. WE LIVED IN OLD CARS AND DIRTY HOTELS, AND WE ATE WHEN WE COULD.

LORETTA LYNN
Singer-songwriter

MUSIC ROW

In Nashville, Tennessee, Music Row is where you'll find the world's largest country music recording companies— along with a huge concentration of recording studios and music publishing houses.

NASHVILLE SOUND

Developed in the 1950s, Music Row is where you will find RCA's famous Studio B, where Elvis Presley recorded, as well as Columbia's Quonset Hut, where Bob Dylan and Johnny Cash recorded. It is also where Chet Baker developed the famous Nashville Sound, a smooth and sophisticated crossover style of country.

THE GRAND OLE OPRY

Home to the oldest radio station to broadcast in U.S. history

★ ★ ★ ★ ★ ★ ★ ★ ★ ★ ★

The Grand Ole Opry

is renowned today for playing country music, but it originally played opera and symphonic music when it was known as the WSM Barn Dance. In 1927, "Harmonica Wizard" DeFord Bailey became the first African-American performer to be heard on the radio station when he played "Pan American Blues" at the opening of an hour-long show. Afterward, George Hay announced, "For the past hour we have been listening to music taken largely from grand opera; from now on we will present 'The Grand Ole Opry.'" And the rest is history.

⭐ ⭐ ⭐ ⭐ ⭐ ⭐ ⭐ ⭐ ⭐

WSM BARN DANCE

The Grand Ole Opry started life as the WSM Barn Dance, a radio show launched by the National Life and Accident Insurance Company. The small studio in its Nashville office even had a window so people walking past it in the hall could see inside. It first aired on October 25, 1925, with the logo WSM, an acronym for the company slogan: "We Shield Millions."

⭐ ⭐ ⭐ ⭐ ⭐ ⭐ ⭐ ⭐ ⭐

THE GRAND OLE OPRY HAS INDUCTED MORE THAN 200 MEMBERS.

From Hank Williams to Patsy Cline, Garth Brooks to Martina McBride, Carrie Underwood to Luke Combs, the Grand Ole Opry's membership list is a who's who of country music legends and stars. Membership is not a posthumous honor, but being asked to join the Opry is still considered one of the highest achievements in country music.

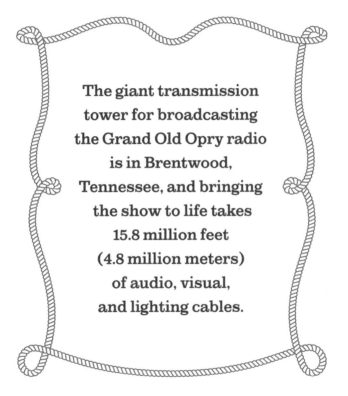

The giant transmission
tower for broadcasting
the Grand Old Opry radio
is in Brentwood,
Tennessee, and bringing
the show to life takes
15.8 million feet
(4.8 million meters)
of audio, visual,
and lighting cables.

Out of about 15,000 radio stations broadcasting in the United States, about 2,100 stations specialize in country music, which is more than any other type of music format. These radio stations, country music listeners' main source for listening to their preferred music, are particularly influential in the country music industry.

ON THE MOVE

The Grand Ole Opry expanded from being a radio station to having the "country's most famous stage." It has moved home five times.

October 3, 1934
The Opry moved to The Belcourt Theatre, a small community playhouse near Vanderbilt University. Because the venue was so small, artists sometimes performed twice a day.

June 13, 1936
The Opry was staged at the Dixie Tabernacle, a rustic religious meeting hall in East Nashville.

June 1939

It was here, in the elegant neoclassical
War Memorial Auditorium, that the
Opry began to charge 25 cents for entry.
However, rowdy fans would force the
Opry to find a new home.

June 1943

The Opry moved to the Ryman Auditorium,
with 2,300 seats. It would become known
as the "Mother Church of Country Music."
(The Opry returns every winter for a
special run.)

March 15, 1974

When the Opry moved to the Grand Ole
Opry House, a 6-foot (1.8-meter)-diameter
circle of wood was removed from the stage
at the Ryman Auditorium and is now part
of the new theater.

OPENING NUMBER

One of the Grand Ole Opry performers, back in 1974, was President Richard Nixon, who played "God Bless America" on the piano at the opening of the current theater.

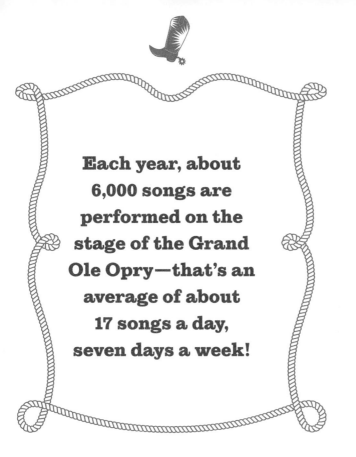

Each year, about 6,000 songs are performed on the stage of the Grand Ole Opry—that's an average of about 17 songs a day, seven days a week!

"

WHAT I GOTTEN TO OBSERVE
IN THE COUPLE OF YEARS I HAVE
KNOWN YOU IS HOW GENUINE YOU
ARE. I THINK COUNTRY MUSIC IS IN
GOOD HANDS. YOU ARE EXACTLY
THE KIND OF ARTIST THAT THE OPRY
LOVES . . . EVERYBODY TONIGHT
SAYS HOW DESERVING YOU ARE
AND IT'S ABOUT TIME.

"

TRISHA YEARWOOD

On inducting Lauren Alaina, the youngest inductee into
the Grand Ole Opry on February 14, 2022

INTIMATE LISTENING

The Bluebird Café's "listening room" is one of the city's best-loved live music venues, and has only 90 seats. Not only might you catch a hit songwriter in an intimate setting, but you may hear an up-and-coming rising star. There's one rule at the Bluebird: No talking during performances!

COUNTRY MUSIC HALL OF FAME

Created by the Country Music Association in 1961, the Country Music Hall of Fame honors top figures in the world of country music. The first inductees were Hank Williams, Jimmie Rodgers, and Fred Rose. Found in the heart of downtown Nashville, it also houses the largest collection of country music artifacts.

PIGEON FORGE

Found in Tennessee on the doorstep of
the Smoky Mountains, Pigeon Forge
features country shows with dazzling
costumes and flashy special effects—
plus the city includes Dollywood, Dolly
Parton's famous theme park
and childhood home.

TOP 12 U.S. COUNTRY FESTIVALS

Prefer to enjoy your music live than to stream it or listen to the radio? Here's a list of the top-rated festivals.

★ ★ ★ ★ ★ ★ ★ ★ ★ ★ ★

1. **Stagecoach:** California's Country Music Festival: Indio, California
2. **Pepsi Gulf Coast Jam:** Country on the Coast: Panama City Beach, Florida
3. **CMA Music Festival:** Nashville, Tennessee
4. **We Fest:** Detroit Lakes, Minnesota
5. **Watershed Festival:** George, Washington
6. **Country Fest:** Cadott, Wisconsin Brooklyn, Michigan
7. **Faster Horses Country Music Festival:** Brooklyn, Michigan
8. **Rock the South:** Cullman, Alabama
9. **Country LakeShake:** Northerly Island, Chicago, Illinois
10. **Kicker Country Stampede:** Manhattan, Kansas
11. **Taste of Country Music Festival:** Hunter Mountain, New York
12. **Caroline Country Music Fest:** Myrtle Beach, South Carolina

★ ★ ★ ★ ★ ★ ★ ★ ★ ★ ★

TAILGATE
PARTY

Don't want to leave your pickup truck behind? Tailgate Feast, in Norco, California, is described as "the first country music festival that caters to the fans who show up hours before the concert to pop a top, drop a tailgate, and turn the parking lot . . . or acres of lush green grass . . . into the party."

HEAD FOR THE
OZARKS

For those attracted to dazzling shiny
costumes, there might be no better place
to get your toes tapping than in
the Ozarks in Branson, Missouri.
Its 76 Country Boulevard is lined with
theaters where choreographed
country music performances are
staged every day.

Perhaps the most famous country music dance hall in the United States, Broken Spoke in Austin, Texas, is where thousands of eager newbies have learned the Texas two-step. The original bar was first built in 46 days by a 25-year-old James White, who started the building on September 25, 1964.

His reason for building it? He wanted a place to get a cold beer and Southern soul food with a good jukebox. However, he noticed his customers would have to dance outside due to lack of space, so he added the dance hall and bandstand at the back. Famous musicians that have graced the stage include Bob Wills and Willie Nelson, and since the 1980s it has become an icon, visited by tourists from all over the world. White was surprised when two Belgians told him in 1989, "Everyone in Belgium knows about the Broken Spoke."

TOP 12 COUNTRY FESTIVALS WORLDWIDE

Country music festivals aren't just an American thing. Travel around the world and you might be surprised at the number you can visit. These are the best according to ranker.com.

1. **Country Thunder:** Saskatchewan, Canada
2. **CMC Rocks QLD:** Queensland, Australia
3. **Tamworth Country Music Festival:** New South Wales, Australia
4. **Groundwater Country Music Festival:** Queensland, Australia
5. **Crash My Playa:** Cancun, Mexico
6. **Boots and Hearts:** Ontario, Canada
7. **Calgary Stampede:** Calgary, Canada
8. **C2C: Country to Country:** London, England; Dublin, Ireland; Glasgow, Scotland; Stockholm, Sweden; Amsterdam, the Netherlands; Berlin, Germany; Sydney and Brisbane, Australia
9. **Cavendish Beach Music Festival:** Cavendish, Canada
10. **Tussock Country Music Festival:** Gore, New Zealand
11. **Country Bauska:** Bauska, Latvia
12. **Western Piknik:** Wolin, Zachodniopomorskie, Poland

According to statistics presented by the Country Music Association, 39% of U.K. adults listen to country music, with almost a third starting to listen to the genre in the past five years. Of new listeners, 64% are Millennials.

Australia has the third-
biggest country fans in the
world, just behind the U.S.
and Canada. According to
Spotify, Keith Urban is the
most-streamed country
artist born outside
the U.S.

CHAPTER 4

THE HITS AND HITMAKERS

There are so many country music
artists, songwriters, producers, and
general talent that it's difficult to choose
the best, but here's a look at the earliest
hitmakers of country as well as a
few recent stars.

LONG-TIME HITS

Some songs have been popular for centuries. "East Virginia" has been recorded by many country musicians, but the melody actually comes from a song known in 17th-century England. "We Shall Overcome" is another popular folk song, but this one has its beginnings in spirituals sung by slaves working on plantations.

THE FIRST HIT SONG

The first commercially made record was by Eck Robertson, recorded on the Victor Records label in 1922, with "Arkansas Traveler" and "Sallie Gooden." However, it was Vernon Dalhart who had the first national country hit, with "Wreck of the Old '97," in 1924.

FIDDLIN' TO THE TOP

The first country musician to have a commercial success was Fiddlin' John Carson, when he recorded two songs in 1923: "The Little Old Log Cabin in the Lane" and "The Old Hen Cackled and the Rooster's Going to Crow."

FATHER OF COUNTRY MUSIC

This title has been earned by Jimmie Rodgers, who is credited with selling the first million copies of a single: "Blue Yodel No. 1." Best known for his unusual style of yodeling, he made numerous recordings between 1927 and 1933, before his untimely death due to tuberculosis.

THE FIRST COUNTRY STARS

The most popular old-time music recordings of the late 1920s were from the Carter Family, a trio consisting of A. P. Carter, his wife Sarah, and his sister-in-law Maybelle. The three sang in harmony while Sarah played autoharp and Maybelle played guitar. Their hit songs include "Keep on the Sunny Side" and "Wildwood Flower."

THE SINGING COWBOY

Gene Autry was known as the "Singing Cowboy" for a good reason. During the 1930s and 1940s, he appeared in 93 movies as well as hosting his own TV program, *The Gene Autry Show*. He personified the straight-shooting and honest hero that millions of Americans grew to love.

KING OF THE COWBOYS

When Leonard Franklin Skye signed his first contract with Republic Pictures, they wanted a rugged cowboy character, so changed his name to Roy Rogers, who would become known as the "King of the Cowboys." A shy introvert who dropped out of school for being teased, as Roy Rogers he was a star on the silver screen, part of it with his horse Trigger, for more than 50 years. He made two to eight movies a year from 1935-51, and starred with his wife Dale Evans in *The Roy Rogers Show* from 1951-57.

Trigger starred with Roy in almost 90 movies and 100 episodes of the singer's show. Trigger also had a name change. The horse was once called Golden Cloud and in his first appearance was in 1938 in *The Adventures of Robin Hood*, ridden by Maid Marian.

TOP OF THE CHARTS

Eddy Arnold was one of country music's favorite singers in the late 1940s and early 1950s. His 1947 song "I'll Hold You in My Heart (Till I Can Hold You in My Arms)" stayed at the No. 1 spot for 21 weeks, a record that he held for more than 60 years. He also held a record 28 No. 1 songs until it was broken in 1980.

OUTLAW WILLIE NELSON

The country singer's first song—written at the age of seven—was about a golden star sticker that his grandmother would give him during music lessons. One of his most famous songs, "On the Road Again," was written on a sick bag while on an airplane—it won Grammy Award for Best Country Song in 1981.

THE MAN IN BLACK

Johnny Cash was one of country music's biggest stars of all time, combining rockabilly with honky-tonk. Instead of wearing cowboy clothes, he opted to wear black, hence his nickname. However, he wasn't the only one to make this fashion statement: Roy Orbison also chose to wear black, as well as a pair of dark sunglasses.

A BOY NAMED...

Johnny Cash is known for singing "A Boy Named Sue," but he didn't write the song. Poet, author, and songwriter Shel Silverstein wrote it, as well as a number of other songs for top country singers, including Bobby Bare, Kris Kristofferson, Waylon Jennings, and Emmylou Harris.

DECADES
OF
DOLLY

Everyone loves Dolly Parton,
one of the best-ever female country
singers. This petite powerhouse
holds a number of well-deserved
records in country music.

- **The most top 10 albums on the *Billboard* Top Country Albums chart.**
- **The most No. 1 hits by a female artist on the *Billboard* Hot Country Songs chart.**
- **The only artist to have top 20 hits in every decade, from the 1960s to the 2010s, on the *Billboard* Hot Country Songs chart.**

(Dolly had previously held the record for the most top 10 hits by a female country artist, but that was broken in 2009 by Reba McEntire.)

TOP 10 U.S. COUNTRY ARTISTS

Statistics for Country Radio Seminar 2022 found the following artists made the most appearances on Amazon Music Charts. It might be surprising who didn't make the list!

1. Taylor Swift
2. Eagles
3. John Denver
4. ZZ Top
5. Alan Jackson
6. Johnny Cash
7. Tom Petty
8. Morgan Wallen
9. Luke Combs
10. Creedence Clearwater

JOHN DENVER

The first person to be inducted in the Colorado Music Hall of Fame, John Denver's real name is Henry John Deutschendorf Jr. and he is known for hits like "Leaving on a Jet Plane," "Take Me Home, Country Roads," and "Annie's Song." His ashes were scattered over the Rocky Mountains.

ALABAMA

The country music band, from Alabama
unsurprisingly, consisted of three
cousins who survived on tip jars for
six years before signing their first
major record deal. They become one
of the 1970s best-selling acts with
more than 40 No. 1 country hits on the
Billboard charts and selling over
75 million records.

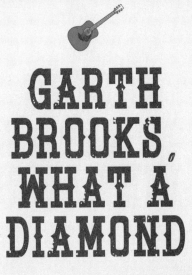

GARTH BROOKS, WHAT A DIAMOND

Top album sales goes to Garth Brooks, who has sold more than any other performer, with 180 million records sold worldwide, and 157 million of them in the U.S. alone. Nine of Garth's albums have been given Diamond status from the RIAA (Recording Industry Association of America).

ACHING TOWARD A LINE DANCE

Line dancing to country music, like the music itself, has its roots in folk, but it wasn't until the 1970s that it became a popular trend with such dances as "Cowboy Boogie" and the "Walkin' Wazi." However, it was "Achy Breaky Heart," sung by Billy Ray Cyrus, hitting the charts in 1992, that made line dancing so popular.

REBA AND MIRANDA SWAP RECORDS

Reba McEntire—the only country female solo act to have a No. 1 hit in four straight decades, from the 1980s to the 2010s—held the record for the most ACM Awards for Female Vocalist of the Year until Miranda Lambert stole that title in 2018.

TRAVIS'S 40+ CLUB

Blues Brothers actor Travis Tritt is no stranger to the Hot Country Songs charts, having entered it more than 40 times. As well as having 20 top 10 hits, five of Travis's songs have made it to No. 1. He's also been awarded seven platinum or higher albums, with one reaching triple-platinum status.

TOP 10 GREATEST COUNTRY HITS

Here's a list of the best country songs of the 20th century.

1. **"Jolene"**
   by Dolly Parton
2. **"I Walk the Line"**
   by Johnny Cash
3. **"I'm So Lonesome
   I Could Cry"**
   by Hank Williams
4. **"The Gambler"**
   by Kenny Rogers
5. **"Crazy"** by Patsy Cline

6. **"The Dance"**
   by Garth Brooks
7. **"Witchita Lineman"**
   by Glen Campbell
8. **"On the Road Again"**
   by Willie Nelson
9. **"Stand by Your Man"**
   by Tammy Wynette
10. **"Okie from Muskogee"**
    by Merle Haggard

SHANIA IS OVER THE TOP

With more than 100 million records being sold, Shania Twain has made history as the best-selling female artist in country music, placing her firmly among the top-selling music artists of all time. Her third album, *Come On Over*, released in 1997, sold more than 40 million copies worldwide.

LORETTA'S MEDAL OF FREEDOM

Not only is Loretta Lynn the most awarded female artist in country music, but she was also given the Presidential Medal of Freedom by President Barack Obama for her courageous work in breaking barriers in a male-dominated industry.

TAYLOR SWIFT A NO. 1 WRITER

When Taylor Swift wrote "Our Song," she was only 14 years of age. Not only did she play it at her ninth-grade talent show in school, but it became a No. 1 hit on the charts.

"

I THINK THE FIRST THING
YOU SHOULD KNOW IS THAT
NOBODY IN COUNTRY MUSIC
'MADE IT' THE SAME WAY. IT'S
ALL DIFFERENT. THERE'S NO
BLUEPRINT FOR SUCCESS . . .

"

TAYLOR SWIFT
Singer-songwriter

TOP 5 COUNTRY VIDEOS

As of 2022, these are the most-viewed country music videos on YouTube with number of views.

1. **Taylor Swift** "You Belong with Me" — 989 million
2. **Florida Georgia Line, featuring Bebe Rexha** "Meant to Be" — 828 million
3. **Taylor Swift** "Love Story" — 490 million
4. **Chris Stapleton** "Tennessee Whiskey" — 380 million
5. **Lady Antebellum** "Need You Now" — 330 million

TOP 10 COUNTRY ALBUMS

According to the Country Radio Seminar 2022, these are the top 10 country radio tracks.

1. **"We Didn't Have Much"** by Justin Moore
2. **"I Hope"** by Gabby Barrett
3. **"Beers and Sunshine"** by Darius Rucker
4. **"Willow"** by Taylor Swift
5. **"What's Your Country Song"** by Thomas Rhett
6. **"Forever After All"** by Luke Combs
7. **"Single Saturday Night"** by Cole Swindell
8. **"Fancy Like"** by Walker Hayes
9. **"One of Them Girls"** by Lee Brice
10. **"Gone"** by Dierks Bentley

CHAPTER 5

BANJOS, GUITARS, AND MORE

From the zither to the guitar, country musicians have specific preferences for the instrument they play—and not just the type of instrument but the specific instrument itself.

OLD-TIME INSTRUMENTS

European immigrants who settled
in the American South brought their
fiddles (or violins) with them, and
they were joined by musicians playing
the banjo. After World War I, the
dulcimer, autoharp, and guitar would be
incorporated into the genre.

FROM
BANJAR
TO BANJO

The banjo is a string instrument derived
from an African instrument with
similar names: *banjar, banju, bania*. It
has a hoop-shaped body with a piece
of vellum stretched over the frame,
somewhat like a tambourine, and like a
violin or guitar, strings are attached to
a tailpiece and neck. Initially, banjos had
four strings but later models have five
to nine strings.

ZITHER

Any stringed instrument for playing music, with up to 40 gut or metal strings of the same length as the instrument's soundboard, can be called a zither. Zithers are placed on the lap for playing and are plucked, but some types can be bowed.

APPALACHIAN DULCIMER

The Appalachian dulcimer is a zither that has its beginnings in the dulcimer that probably arrived in central Europe from Persia in the 1400s. This string instrument is a member of the lute family, with a body that extends along the fretted fingerboard and that is fitted with three to five metal strings.

AUTOHARP

An autoharp, or autochord, is a
strummed or plucked instrument that
is similar in construction to a zither.
However, it uses buttons to play chords
by dampening the strings not being
played. It first appeared in the late
19th century, when it became part of
American folk and eventually
country and bluegrass.

THE BOWED FIDDLE

From the German *fiedel* or French *vielle*, the fiddle is the precursor to the violin. This bowed, string instrument first appeared in Europe in the 10th century and may have been derived from the *rabab*, an earlier Arab bowed instrument.

KITCHEN INSTRUMENTS

The instruments in a jug band not
only included a bass or bull fiddle but
also a jug and washboard, stovepipes,
spoons, bones, and even a comb.
The mouth organ, aka harmonica,
was also part of the band, because
it was easy to transport. Jug bands were
popular among soldiers and cowboys
in rural areas.

OUD TO LUTE TO GUITAR

The North African oud, a bowl-shaped string instrument with a short neck, was the forerunner of the lute, a string instrument with a pear-shaped body that has a fretted fingerboard with six to 13 pairs of strings, which could be tuned by turning pegs. The guitar evolved from the lute in medieval Europe.

LUTHIER

The term "lute" comes from the French *luth*, and a luthier originally referred to a lute maker. However, the word has evolved to be used for anyone making stringed instruments, including violins, and someone who makes guitars is known as a luthier. Among the best luthiers in the U.S. are C. F. Martin and Orville Gibson.

EARLY AMERICAN GUITARS

When European immigrants arrived in the U.S., their classical acoustic guitars had gut strings. Some of them were luthiers, who adapted how they made instruments to their new country. C. F. Martin was one of these, who developed X bracing to strengthen the soundboard.

FIRST FOLK GUITARS

As folk music gained in popularity in the early 20th century, the musicians needed guitars that could play louder to larger crowds. Steel strings were introduced about 1900, which had a twangy sound that was perfect for playing at barn dances.

FLATTOP VERSUS ARCHTOP

The European guitar evolved into the flattop guitar, named for the soundboard, which is also known as the "top." In the 1890s, Orville Gibson introduced the archtop, with f-holes instead of a sound hole and an adjustable bridge that made it possible to play this guitar louder than a flattop.

MAYBELLE'S GIBSON L-5

Orville Gibson introduced the Gibson L-5 in 1922, a large guitar with a loud sound and beautiful tones. Mother Maybelle, of the Carter Family, played this guitar with a simple fingering style, using her thumb to play the bass strings and strumming chords on the upper strings. This would become known as the Carter Scratch.

"

I WAS 12 WHEN I ORDERED MY
FIRST GUITAR OUT OF THE WORN
AND DISCOLORED PAGES OF THE
SEARS AND ROEBUCK CATALOG.
THE STORY THAT I BOUGHT IT
ON THE INSTALLMENT PLAN IS
UNTRUE . . . I PAD CASH, $8, MONEY
I HAD SAVED AS A HIRED HAND
ON MY UNCLE CALVIN'S FARM,
BALING AND STACKING HAY.

"

GENE AUTRY
Singer-songerwriter and actor

BLUEGRASS VIRTUOSO

Although he would have greater fame as a member of the Byrds in the 1960s, Clarence White was a virtuoso guitar player who was the first to introduce solo guitar playing to bluegrass music while playing with the Kentucky Colonels. Clarence played a Martin D-28, acquired second hand in a guitar store in 1959, and also a modified 1950s Telecaster, the first ever "pull-string" or B-Bender guitar.

TONY RICE AND THE MARTIN D-28

Perhaps one of the most influential guitar players of his time in the bluegrass genre, Tony Rice was so heavily influenced by Clarence White's playing that he acquired his famous Martin guitar, which had been shot by a pellet gun. He restored and played it to the end of his career.

OPRY BAN

Until the 1940s, electric guitars and amps were banned in the Grand Ole Opry; the restriction was relaxed after Ernest Tubb played one. Percussion and horns were strictly banned, and drums remained frowned upon until the 1970s. In 1944, Bob Wills had a drum set pushed onstage for a single song. Wills never played for the Opry again.

PIANO KEYS

When you listen to country music, you don't often hear a piano. The piano wasn't an original instrument for creating country music, only being introduced to the genre in the 1930s. Today, musicians more often use either an electric piano or synthesizer.

"IF YOU'RE GONNA PLAY IN TEXAS . . ."

A 1984 country song by the group Alabama is a good reminder that the guitar isn't the only instrument in a band. "If You're Gonna Play in Texas (You Gotta Have a Fiddle in the Band)" has lyrics reminding musicians of the importance of a fiddle.

GIBSON
LES PAUL

Les Paul might have been a famous jazz musician, but his collaboration with Gibson led to the development of the Gibson Les Paul. This electric guitar was designed to deliver a heavy tone with a midrange punch, making it perfect for big country rock. It's behind the sounds of The Allman Brothers and Lynyrd Skynyrd.

66

ALL I'VE GOT IS A RED GUITAR, THREE CHORDS, AND THE TRUTH.

99

HARLAND HOWARD
Country music songwriter

FENDER TELECASTER

The first mass-produced electric guitar was designed by Leo Fender in the early 1950s. Since his Telecaster, with its twangy sound, was introduced, it has taken country music by storm. Famous guitar players strumming their stuff on a Tele include Waylon Jennings, Buck Owens, Merle Haggard, Brad Paisley, and Marty Stuart—who plays the original B-Bender Telecaster once owned by Clarence White.

COLLINGS NO. 29

When country singer-songwriter Lyle Lovett met Bill Collings, a respected luthier, in 1978, the guitar maker described the market at the time: "Well, you have your Martins and you have your Gibsons, and that's it." Lovett ordered a Collings guitar, which was based on a Martin-style Dreadnought. It was the 29th guitar made by Collings, hence the No. 29.

MERLE TRAVIS'S PAUL BIGSBY NO. 2

When country musician Merle Travis took his Gibson guitar to Paul Bigsby, a designer of motorcycle engines, to fix a tuning problem in the late 1940s, he walked away with a new tailpiece now known as the Bigsby vibrato tailpiece, or whammy bar. The collaboration between the two men led to the Paul Bigsby No. 2, now a legendary solid-body electric guitar.

WILLIE'S MARTIN N-20

Willie Nelson has used the same Martin N-20 guitar—named Trigger (after Roy Rogers' horse)—for more than 50 years. In that time he has played his guitar in more than 10,000 shows. He bought it in Nashville from a guitarist named Shot Jackson in 1969.

THE COUNTRYMAN GUITAR

The Gretsch 6120 was the result of
a collaboration in the 1950s between
Jimmie Webster, a designer at Gretsch,
and the musician Chet Atkins. Webster
had wanted cowboy details on the
guitar but Atkins was adamant that it
was unadorned. The guitar had been
designed to reduce feedback, so the
black f-holes seen on the guitar
are only paint.

THE FENDER STRATOCASTER

After the success of the Telecaster, Leo Fender began working on a new design with Freddie Travares, a local guitarist. They came up with the legendary Fender Stratocaster, with a new body shape, a new, refined vibrato device, and three pickups, in 1961. When Keith Urban was looking for an amp in a guitar store in Sydney, Australia, he picked up a black 1964 Fender Stratocaster to try out the amp—and it has become his favorite guitar.

66

ONLY IN COUNTRY MUSIC CAN
YOU COMPARE AN OLD PICKUP
TRUCK AND AN OLD GUITAR TO
YOUR WIFE AND TURN IT INTO
A LOVE SONG.

99

DIERKS BENTLEY
Musician and singer-songwriter

★ ★ ★ ★ ★ ★ ★ ★ ★ ★

CHAPTER 6

HEARTS
ON
SLEEVES

Quotes, sayings, and words of wisdom
from the greats, who have often tapped
into their life experiences in the
creation of their music.

★ ★ ★ ★ ★ ★ ★ ★ ★ ★

"

I ALWAYS HAD A STANDARD OF, BACK
WHEN I WAS DOING THE COUNTRY
MUSIC, I ALWAYS TOLD PEOPLE I
WOULD NEVER RECORD A SONG THAT
I WOULDN'T SIT DOWN AND SING IN
FRONT OF MY MOM AND DAD.

"

RICKY SKAGGS

Singer and musician

"

TRUE COUNTRY MUSIC IS HONESTY, SINCERITY, AND REAL LIFE TO THE HILT.

"

GARTH BROOKS

Singer-songwriter

GENE AUTRY'S COWBOY CODE

The Singing Cowboy had a cowboy code that is still valid today, whether you're a cowboy or cowgirl, or not.

1. A cowboy must never shoot first, hit a smaller man, or take unfair advantage.

2. He must never go back on his word or a trust confided in him.

3. He must always tell the truth.

4. He must be gentle with children, the elderly, and animals.

5. He must not advocate or possess racially or religiously intolerant ideas.

6. He must help people in distres

7. He must be a good worker.

8. He must keep himself clean in thought, speech, action, and personal habits.

9. He must respect women, parents, and his nation's laws

10. The cowboy is a patriot.

GOING SEPARATE WAYS

Jimmie Rodgers traveled with his band
the Tenneva Ramblers in 1927 to Bristol,
Tennessee. However, when he got there,
Rodgers had a huge argument with his
band and they kicked him out. Both the
Tenneva Ramblers and Jimmie Rodgers
were recorded on that day, separately,
but only Rodgers would become a star.

> **"**

I LOVE SONGS ABOUT HORSES, RAILROADS, LAND, JUDGMENT DAY, FAMILY, HARD TIMES, WHISKEY, COURTSHIP, MARRIAGE, ADULTERY, SEPARATION, MURDER, WAR, PRISON, RAMBLING, DAMNATION, HOME, SALVATION, DEATH, PRIDE, HUMOR, PIETY, REBELLION, PATRIOTISM, LARCENY, DETERMINATION, TRAGEDY, ROWDINESS, HEARTBREAK, AND LOVE. AND MOTHER. AND GOD.

> **"**

JOHNNY CASH
Musician and singer-songwriter

YOU'VE GOT TO CARE ABOUT THE
MUSIC . . . YOU'D BETTER NOT BE DOING
IT FOR THE PUBLICITY, THE FAME, OR
THE MONEY. AND YOU'D SURE BETTER
NOT BE DOING IT BECAUSE IT'S A WAY
TO MAKE A LIVING, 'CAUSE THAT AIN'T
ALWAYS GOING TO BE EASY. YOU GOT
TO BELIEVE IT, BELIEVE IN THE MUSIC.
YOU GOT TO MEAN IT.

WAYLON JENKINS
Musician and singer-songwriter

"

A LOT OF COUNTRY MUSIC IS SAD.
I THINK MOST ART COMES OUT
OF POVERTY AND HARD TIMES. IT
APPLIES TO MUSIC. THREE CHORDS
AND THE TRUTH—THAT'S WHAT A
COUNTRY SONG IS. THERE IS A LOT OF
HEARTACHE IN THE WORLD.

"

WILLIE NELSON
Musician and singer-songwriter

WILLIE AND THE IRS

The Internal Revenue Service (IRS) claimed that Willie Nelson owed $32 million in taxes. Nelson's lawyer managed to reduce the amount to $6 million, but Nelson wouldn't pay up. To settle his debt, he released a double album, *The IRS Tapes: Who'll Buy My Memories?*, with all profits going to the IRS. His debt was cleared in 1993.

"

ROGER MILLER OPENED A LOT OF
PEOPLE'S EYES TO THE POSSIBILITIES
OF COUNTRY MUSIC, AND IT'S MAKING
MORE IMPACT NOW BECAUSE IT'S
EARTHY MATERIAL: STORIES AND
THINGS THAT HAPPEN TO EVERYDAY
PEOPLE. I CALL IT 'PEOPLE MUSIC.'

"

GLEN CAMPBELL
Guitarist and singer-songwriter

PRISON
RECORD

Johnny Cash played two live shows
in January 1968 at the Folsom Prison,
California, which were released on the
At Folsom Prison album. Although he
spent a night in jail a few times after
being arrested for minor misdemeanors,
he never served a sentence. On one
occasion, in 1965, he was arrested for
picking flowers on private property in
Starkville, Mississippi.

I WALK THE LINE

Johnny Cash had a romantic side to him, and when he wrote the lyrics in "I Walk the Line," he was writing about his love for Vivian, his first wife. However, the unusual progression in the chords came from a previous accident— they were inspired by the sounds played on a cassette tape that had somehow got turned around and played his music backward.

66

THERE'S A NEW HIT ROCK
GROUP OR SINGER EVERY
FIVE MINUTES, BUT WITH
COUNTRY MUSIC, YOU HAVE
ONE HIT AND THOSE PEOPLE
LOVE YOU FOREVER.

KENNY ROGERS
Musician and singer-songwriter

DON'T CHANGE YOUR VOICE

When Johnny Cash was growing up, his mother (who played guitar and piano) sent him to singing lessons, but his teacher told the young Johnny to quit, saying, "Don't ever take voice lessons again." This wasn't because of his ability to sing but because of his unique style of singing. She told him, "Don't let me or anyone change how you sing."

CHANGE
YOUR VOICE

Bob Dylan is recognized for his folk singing, but when he quit smoking in 1969, there was a change in his voice that apparently was good for country music. Kris Kristofferson described him as opening "the doors in Nashville when he did *Blonde on Blonde* and *Nashville Skyline*. The country scene was so conservative until he arrived. He brought in a whole new audience."

66

BUT YA KNOW WHAT, I AM A PART OF SOMETHING THAT HAPPENED. I'M A PART OF THE MUSIC THAT HAPPENED. MY VOICE IS ONE MORE INSTRUMENT, IS WHAT IT IS.

99

WAYLON JENNINGS
Singer-songwriter

YOUR CHEATIN' HEART

Many of Hank Williams' songs were written by his publisher Fred Rose, who would complete songs after Williams handed him an outline and some phrases. By 1952, Williams' drinking problem led to him being dropped by Rose. Williams wrote "Your Cheatin' Heart" and recorded it in September 1952, a few months before he died.

MY SECOND WIFE BONNIE OWENS
AND I WORKED TOGETHER AFTER
WE DIVORCED FOR A PERIOD OF
MAYBE 20 YEARS. AND I MANAGED
TO STAY FRIENDS WITH ANOTHER
WIFE. AND THEN THERE'S ONE THAT
I DON'T MESS WITH. EVERYBODY'S
GOT ONE OF THOSE.

MERLE HAGGARD
Singer-songwriter

> **"**
>
> NINETY-NINE PERCENT OF THE
> WORLD'S LOVERS ARE NOT WITH
> THEIR FIRST CHOICE.
> THAT'S WHAT MAKES THE
> JUKEBOX PLAY.
>
> **"**

WILLIE NELSON
Musician and singer-songwriter

TOP 10 COUNTRY CHRISTMAS SONGS

Here's some of country's favorite Christmas songs.

1. **"Christmas Isn't Canceled (Just You)"**
   by Kelly Clarkson

2. **"I Saw Mommy Kissing Santa Claus"**
   by Dolly Parton

3. **"Christmas in Dixie"**
   by Alabama

4. **"Country Christmas"**
   by Loretta Lynn

5. **"Last Christmas"**
   by Taylor Swift

6. **"Dear Santa"**
   by Tim McGraw

7. **"Take Me Home for Christmas"**
   by Dan and Shay

8. **"Santa Looked a Lot Like Daddy"**
   by Brad Paisley

9. **"Joy to the World"**
   by Faith Hill

10. **"Baby It's Cold Outside"**
    by Garth Brooks and Trisha Yearwood

PLEDGE TO COUNTRY MUSIC

In March 1964, Buck Owens posted a full-page ad in *Music City News* to support respect of country music:

"I shall sing no song that is not a country song. I shall make no record that is not a country record. I refuse to be known as anything but a country singer. I am proud to be associated with country music. Country music and country fans made me what I am today. And I shall not forget it."

"

I'VE ALWAYS SAID MUSIC
SHOULD MAKE YOU LAUGH,
MAKE YOU CRY, OR MAKE
YOU THINK.

KENNY ROGERS
Musician and singer-songwriter

66

FOR ME, SINGING SAD SONGS
OFTEN HAS A WAY OF
HEALING A SITUATION. IT
GETS THE HURT OUT IN THE
OPEN, INTO THE LIGHT, OUT
OF THE DARKNESS.

99

REBA MCENTIRE
Singer-songwriter

> **WHEN SOMETHING IS BOTHERING ME, I WRITE A SONG THAT TELLS MY FEELINGS.**

LORETTA LYNN
Singer-songwriter

POPULARITY CONTEST

We may recognize the name of a country singer, but does that mean we like them? According to a YouGov America survey, the following country music artists came out in the top 20 based on two criteria: If people had a positive opinion of the artist (popularity) and if they had heard of the artist (fame).

Artist	Popularity	Fame
1 **Dolly Parton**	78%	95%
2 **Johnny Cash**	71%	95%
3 **Reba McEntire**	64%	92%
4 **Kenny Rogers**	63%	91%
5 **Willie Nelson**	61%	91%
6 **Shania Twain**	60%	90%
7 **Huey Lewis**	59%	82%
8 **Garth Brooks**	59%	93%
9 **John Denver**	58%	85%
10 **Patsy Cline**	58%	83%
11 **Carrie Underwood**	57%	95%
12 **Tim McGraw**	57%	91%
13 **The Everly Brothers**	56%	80%
14 **Faith Hill**	55%	89%
15 **Loretta Lynn**	55%	84%
16 **Alabama**	54%	83%
17 **Randy Travis**	53%	84%
18 **Keith Urban**	53%	90%
19 **Hank Williams**	52%	83%
20 **Brad Paisley**	52%	88%

"

SOMEONE MIGHT LOOK LIKE AN
OVERNIGHT SUCCESS, BUT THERE'S
A LOT OF HARD WORK THAT GOES
INTO IT, AND RIGHTLY SO. THAT'S
THE WAY IT SHOULD BE. THERE ARE
EXCEPTIONS TO THAT RULE, BUT IN
COUNTRY MUSIC, PEOPLE REALLY
HAVE TO PAY THEIR DUES.

"

FRANKIE BALLARD
Singer-songwriter

66

I THINK EVERY ONCE IN A WHILE
COUNTRY HAS LOST ITS WAY, BUT
FOUND ITS WAY BACK. IT'S ALWAYS
GOING TO DRIFT AWAY FROM THE
TRADITIONAL SIDE, BUT THEN FIND
A WAY TO RETURN. THERE'S ROOM
FOR ALL KINDS OF INFLUENCES, BE
IT POP, BLUES, GOSPEL
OR WHATEVER.

RANDY TRAVIS
Singer-songwriter and guitarist

"

MY MUSIC IS NOT
COUNTRY-WESTERN.
I AM A COUNTRY BOY AND
A LOT OF MY MUSIC HAS A
COUNTRY SOUND TO IT.

"

JOHNNY CASH

The New York Times, September 21, 1969

> **"**
> I THINK COUNTRY MUSIC IS POPULAR—HAS BEEN POPULAR AND WILL ALWAYS BE POPULAR, BECAUSE I THINK A LOT OF REAL PEOPLE [ARE] SINGING ABOUT A LOT OF REAL STUFF ABOUT REAL PEOPLE. AND IT'S SIMPLE ENOUGH FOR PEOPLE TO UNDERSTAND IT.
> **"**

DOLLY PARTON
Singer-songwriter

> **"**
>
> I THINK IT SPEAKS TO OUR BASIC
> FUNDAMENTAL FEELINGS, YOU
> KNOW. OF EMOTIONS, OF LOVE,
> OF BREAKUP, OF LOVE AND HATE
> AND DEATH AND DYING, MAMA,
> APPLE PIE, AND THE WHOLE THING.
> IT COVERS A LOT OF TERRITORY,
> COUNTRY MUSIC DOES.
>
> **"**

JOHNNY CASH
CNN interview, 2002